Anthology of CHILDREN'S SONGS

EDITION

C000264368

ISBN 978-1-61780-568-4

HAL•LEONARD®
CORPORATION

7777 W. BLUEMOUND RD. P.O. BOX 13819 MILWAUKEE, WI 53213

Visit Hal Leonard Online at
www.halleonard.com

ALLEY CAT SONG

Words by JACK HARLEN
Music by FRANK BJORN

He goes on the prowl each night like an al-ley cat,

look-in' for some new de-light like an al-ley cat.

She can't trust him out of sight, there's no doubt of that.
He don't know what "faith-ful" means, there's no doubt of that.

A-TISKET A-TASKET

Traditional

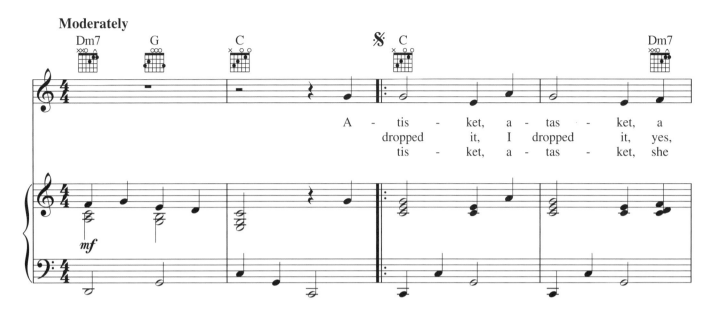

A - tis - ket, a - tas - ket, a
dropped it, I dropped it, yes,
tis - ket, a - tas - ket, she

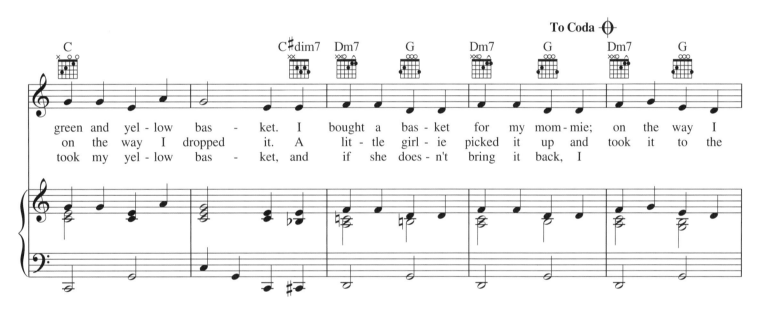

green and yel - low bas - ket. I bought a bas - ket for my mom - mie; on the way I
on the way I dropped it. A lit - tle girl - ie picked it up and took it to the
took my yel - low bas - ket, and if she does - n't bring it back, I

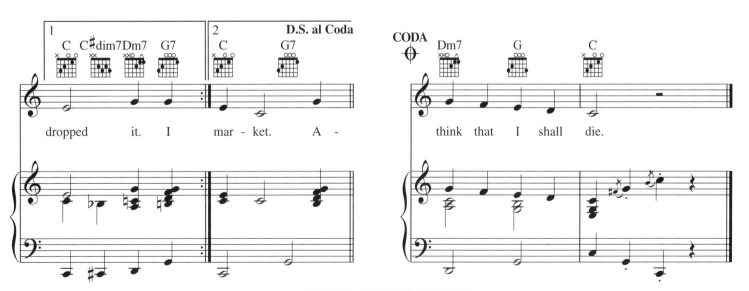

dropped it. I mar - ket. A-

think that I shall die.

ADDAMS FAMILY THEME
Theme from the TV Show and Movie

Music and Lyrics by
VIC MIZZY

They're creep-y and they're kook-y, mys-te-ri-ous and spook-y, they're al-to-geth-er ook-y, the Ad-dams Fam-i-ly. Their house is a mu-se-um, where

ALLEY-OOP

Words and Music by
DALLAS FRAZIER

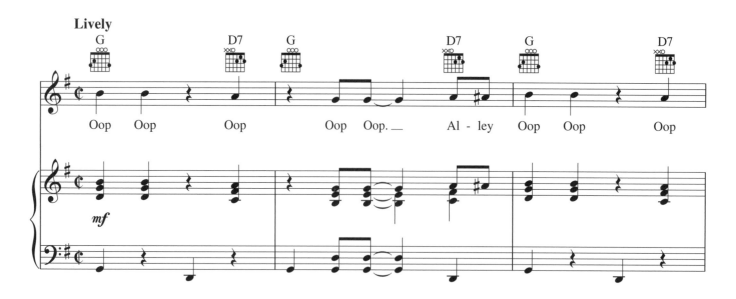

Oop Oop Oop Oop Oop. Al - ley Oop Oop Oop

Oop Oop. There's a man in the fun - ny pa - pers we all know, Al - ley

Oop Oop Oop Oop Oop. He lived way back a

BABY MINE
from Walt Disney's DUMBO

Words by NED WASHINGTON
Music by FRANK CHURCHILL

Moderately slow

Ba - by mine _____ don't you cry. _____

Ba - by mine _____ dry your eye. _____

Rest your head close to my heart, nev-er to part, ba-by of

THE BALLAD OF DAVY CROCKETT

from Walt Disney's DAVY CROCKETT

Words by TOM BLACKBURN
Music by GEORGE BRUNS

Moderately

1. Born on a moun-tain top in Ten - nes - see, green - est state in the
2. eight - een - thir - teen the Creeks up - rose, add - in' red - skin ar - rows to the
3. Off through the woods he's a march - in' a - long, mak - in' up yarns an' a -
4.-10. *(See additional lyrics)*

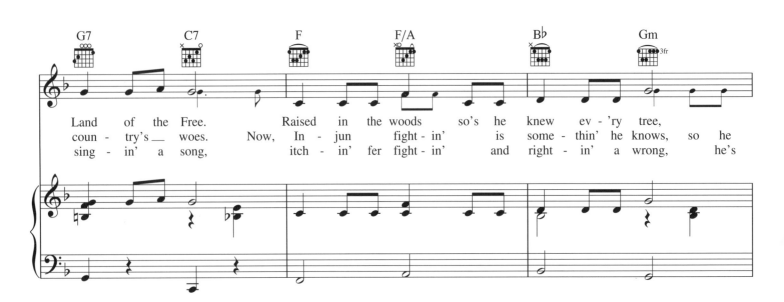

Land of the Free. Raised in the woods so's he knew ev - 'ry tree,
coun - try's __ woes. Now, In - jun fight - in' is some - thin' he knows, so he
sing - in' a song, itch - in' fer fight - in' and right - in' a wrong, he's

kilt him a b'ar when he was on - ly three. Da - vy,
shoul - ders his ri - fle, an' off he ___ goes. Da - vy,
rin - gy as a b'ar, an' twict as ___ strong. Da - vy,

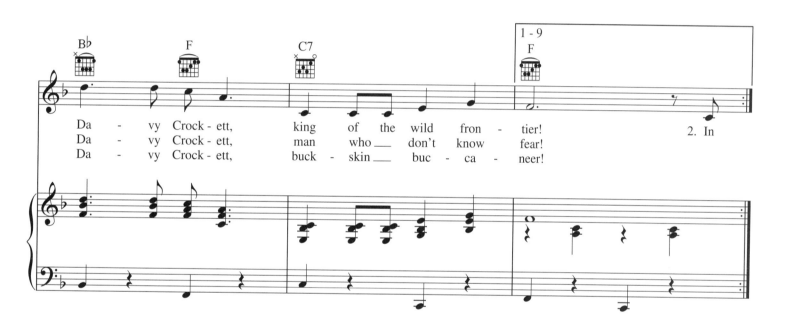

Da - vy Crock - ett, king of the wild fron - tier!
Da - vy Crock - ett, man who ___ don't know fear!
Da - vy Crock - ett, buck - skin ___ buc - ca - neer!

1 - 9

2. In

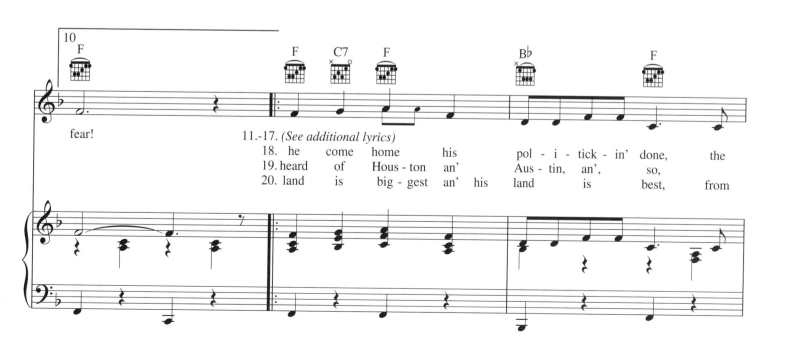

10

fear!

11.-17. *(See additional lyrics)*
18. he come home his pol - i - tick - in' done, the
19. heard of Hous - ton an' Aus - tin, an', so,
20. land is big - gest an' his land is best, from

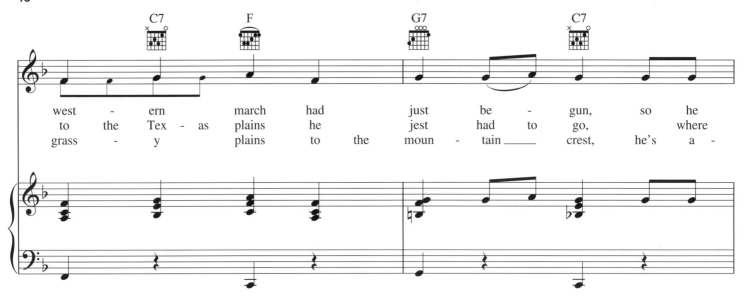

west - ern march had just be - gun, so he
to the Tex - as plains he jest had to go, so where
grass - y plains to the moun - tain _____ crest, he's a -

packed his gear an' his trust - y gun, an' lit out grin - nin' to
Free - dom was fight - in' an - oth - er foe, an' they need - ed him at the
head of us all meet - in' the test, fol - low - in' his leg - end

fol - low the sun. Da - vy, Da - vy Crock - ett,
Al - a - mo. Da - vy, Da - vy Crock - ett,
in - to the West. Da - vy, Da - vy Crock - ett, the

lead - in' the pi - o - neer!
man who ___ don't know fear!
king of the wild fron -

clear!
18. When
19. He
20. His
tier!

Additional Lyrics

4. Andy Jackson is our gen'ral's name,
His reg'lar soldiers we'll put to shame,
Them redskin varmints us Volunteers'll tame,
'Cause we got the guns with the sure-fire aim.
Davy – Davy Crockett,
The champion of us all!

5. Headed back to war from the ol' home place,
But Red Stick was leadin' a merry chase,
Fightin' an' burnin' at a devil's pace
South to the swamps on the Florida Trace.
Davy – Davy Crockett,
Trackin' the redskins down!

6. Fought single-handed through the Injun War
Till the Creeks was whipped an' peace was in store,
An' while he was handlin' this risky chore,
Made hisself a legend forevermore.
Davy – Davy Crockett,
King of the wild frontier!

7. He give his word an' he give his hand
That his Injun friends could keep their land,
An' the rest of his life he took the stand
That justice was due every redskin band.
Davy – Davy Crockett,
Holdin' his promise dear!

8. Home fer the winter with his family,
Happy as squirrels in the ol' gum tree,
Bein' the father he wanted to be,
Close to his boys as the pod an' the pea.
Davy – Davy Crockett,
Holdin' his young 'uns dear!

9. But the ice went out an' the warm winds came
An' the meltin' snow showed tracks of game,
An' the flowers of Spring filled the woods with flame,
An' all of a sudden life got too tame.
Davy – Davy Crockett,
Headin' on West again!

10. Off through the woods we're ridin' along,
Makin' up yarns an' singin' a song.
He's ringy as a b'ar and twice as strong,
An' knows he's right 'cause he ain't often wrong.
Davy – Davy Crockett,
The man who don't know fear!

11. Lookin' fer a place where the air smells clean,
Where the tree is tall an' the grass is green,
Where the fish is fat in an untouched stream,
An' the teemin' woods is a hunter's dream.
Davy – Davy Crockett,
Lookin' fer Paradise!

12. Now he'd lost his love an' his grief was gall.
In his heart he wanted to leave it all,
An' lose himself in the forests tall,
But he answered instead his country's call.
Davy – Davy Crockett,
Beginnin' his campaign!

13. Needin' his help they didn't vote blind,
They put in Davy 'cause he was their kind,
Sent up to Nashville the best they could find,
A fightin' spirit an' a thinkin' mind.
Davy – Davy Crockett,
Choice of the whole frontier!

14. The votes were counted an' he won hands down,
So they sent him off to Washin'ton town
With his best dress suit still his buckskins brown,
A livin' legend of growin' renown.
Davy – Davy Crockett,
The Canebrake Congressman!

15. He went off to Congress an' served a spell,
Fixin' up the Gover'ment an' laws as well,
Took over Washin'ton so we heered tell
An' patched up the crack in the Liberty Bell.
Davy – Davy Crockett,
Seein' his duty clear!

16. Him an' his jokes travelled all through the land,
An' his speeches made him friends to beat the band,
His politickin' was their favorite brand
An' everyone wanted to shake his hand.
Davy – Davy Crockett,
Helpin' his legend grow!

17. He knew when he spoke he sounded the knell
Of his hopes for White House an' fame as well,
But he spoke out strong so hist'ry books tell
An' patched up the crack in the Liberty Bell.
Davy – Davy Crockett,
Seein' his duty clear!

BE OUR GUEST

from Walt Disney's BEAUTY AND THE BEAST

Lyrics by HOWARD ASHMAN
Music by ALAN MENKEN

LUMIERE: *Ma chère Mademoiselle! It is with deepest pride and greatest pleasure that*

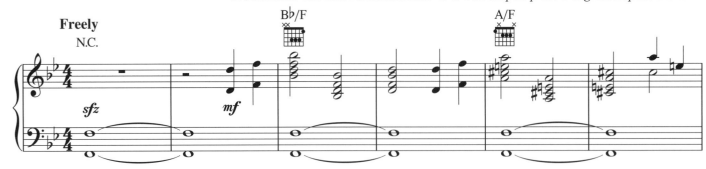

we welcome you here tonight. And now, we invite you to relax. Let us pull up a chair as the dining room proudly presents...

Moderate 2, unhurried

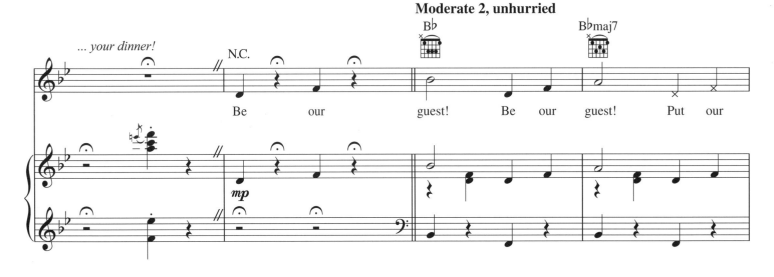

... your dinner!   Be   our   guest!   Be   our   guest!   Put   our

ser - vice to the test. Tie your nap - kin 'round your neck, *cher - ie,* and

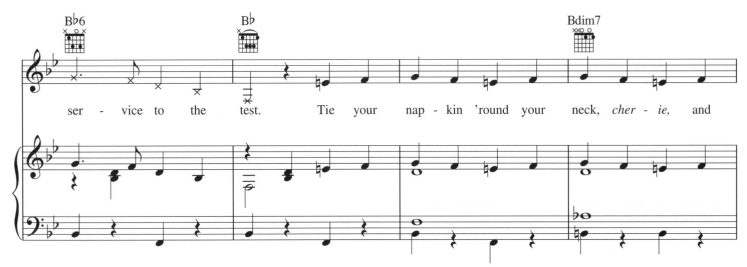

BEIN' GREEN

Words and Music by
JOE RAPOSO

Slowly, reflectively

It's not that eas-y be-in' green,

hav-ing to spend each day the col-or of the leaves, when I think it could be

nic-er be-in' red or yel-low or gold or some-thing much more col-or-ful like

BELLA NOTTE
(This Is the Night)
from Walt Disney's LADY AND THE TRAMP

Words and Music by PEGGY LEE
and SONNY BURKE

This _____ is the night, _____ it's a beau - ti-ful night, _____ and we

call it Bel - la Not - te. Look _____ at the skies; _____ they have

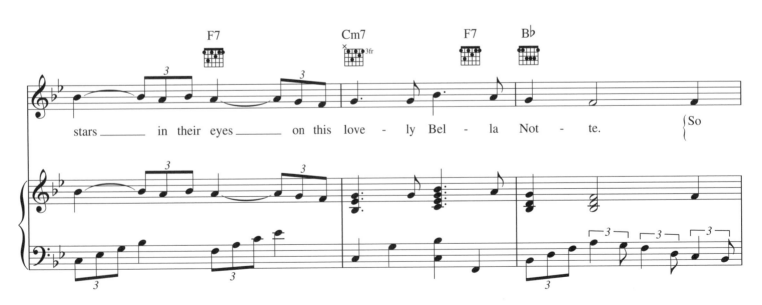

stars _____ in their eyes _____ on this love - ly Bel - la Not - te. {So

THE BIBLE TELLS ME SO

Words and Music by
DALE EVANS

BREAKING FREE

from the Disney Channel Original Movie HIGH SCHOOL MUSICAL

Words and Music by
JAMIE HOUSTON

BROOMSTICK BUCKAROO

Words and Music by GENE AUTRY,
JOHNNY MARVIN and FRANK HARFORD

CANDLE ON THE WATER

from Walt Disney's PETE'S DRAGON

Words and Music by AL KASHA
and JOEL HIRSCHHORN

BUFFALO GALS
(Won't You Come Out Tonight?)

Words and Music by
COOL WHITE (JOHN HODGES)

"C" IS FOR COOKIE

Words and Music by
JOE RAPOSO

Medium slow Ragtime

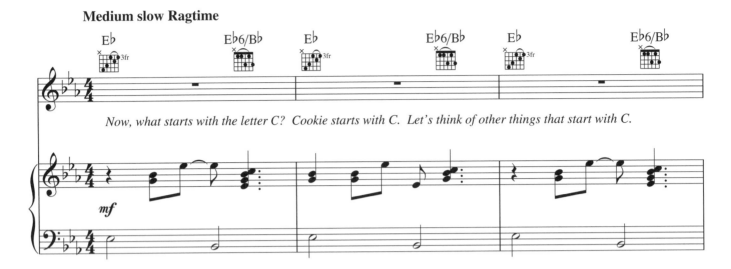

Now, what starts with the letter C? Cookie starts with C. Let's think of other things that start with C.

Ah, who cares about the other things! C is for cook - ie, that's good e - nough for me!
(Spoken:) A round cookie with one bite out of it looks like a C.

C is for cook - ie, that's good e - nough for me! C is for cook - ie, that's
A round doughnut with one bite out of it looks like a C, but it is not as good as a cookie.

THE CANDY MAN
from WILLY WONKA AND THE CHOCOLATE FACTORY

Words and Music by LESLIE BRICUSSE
and ANTHONY NEWLEY

Who can take a sun - rise ____
Who can take a rain - bow ____

sprin - kle it with dew, _____
wrap it in a sigh, _____

cov - er it in choc - 'late and a mir - a - cle or two?
soak it in the sun and make a straw - b'ry lem - on pie?
The

THE CHICKEN DANCE

By TERRY RENDALL
and WERNER THOMAS
English Lyrics by PAUL PARNES

Got a prob-lem? Here's a cure. (We got the cure.) Do the chick-en dance;

make you hap-py for sure. _____ 1.,3. Reach out your arms and

Chorus

swing your part - ner. Make like a bird and

try to fly. Come on out there, you

Additional Lyrics

2. Hey, you're in the swing.
   You're cluckin' like a bird. (Pluck, pluck, pluck, pluck.)
   You're flappin' your wings.
   Don't you feel absurd. (No, no, no, no.)
   It's a chicken dance,
   Like a rooster and a hen. (Ya, ya, ya, ya.)
   Flappy chicken dance;
   Let's do it again. *(To Chorus 2:)*

Chorus 2:
   Relax and let the music move you.
   Let all your inhibitions go.
   Just watch your partner whirl around you.
   We're havin' fun now; I told you so.

3. Now you're flappin' like a bird
   And you're wigglin' too. (I like that move.)
   You're without a care.
   It's a dance for you. (Just made for you.)
   Keep doin' what you do.
   Don't you cop out now. (Don't cop out now.)
   Gets better as you dance;
   Catch your breath somehow.
   Chorus

4. Now we're almost through,
   Really flyin' high. (Bye, bye, bye, bye.)
   All you chickens and birds,
   Time to say goodbye. (To say goodbye.)
   Goin' back to the nest,
   But the flyin' was fun. (Oh, it was fun.)
   Chicken dance was the best,
   But the dance is done.

CHOPSTICKS

By ARTHUR DE LULLI

CIRCLE OF LIFE

from Walt Disney Pictures' THE LION KING

Music by ELTON JOHN
Lyrics by TIM RICE

Relaxed Pop beat

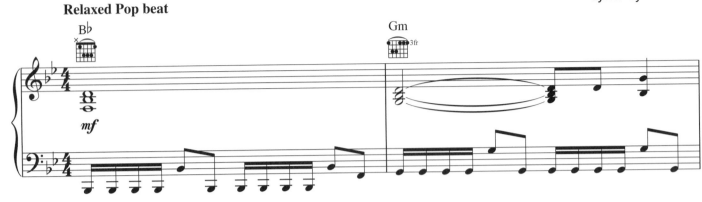

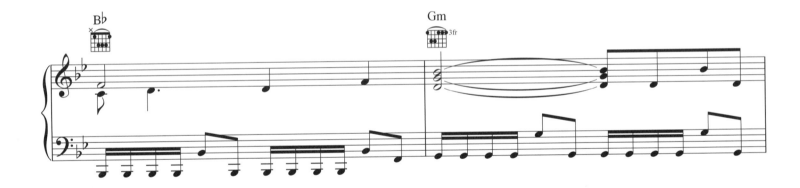

From the

(Oh, My Darling)
CLEMENTINE

Words and Music by
PERCY MONTROSE

dar - ling, oh, my dar - ling Clem-en - tine, you are lost and gone for-

ev - er, dread-ful sor - ry, Clem-en - tine. { Walk - ing tine.
{ She drove

Additional Lyrics

4. Ruby lips above the water,
   Blowing bubbles soft and fine,
   But alas, I was not swimmer,
   Neither was my Clementine.
   Chorus

5. Then the miner, forty-niner,
   Soon began to fret and pine,
   Thought he ought to join his daughter,
   So he's now with Clementine.
   Chorus

6. I'm so lonely, lost without her,
   Wish I'd had a fishing line,
   Which I might have cast about her,
   Might have saved my Clementine.
   Chorus

7. While I'm dreaming, I can see her,
   With a garment soaked in brine,
   Then she rises from the waters,
   And I kiss my Clementine.
   Chorus

COLORS OF THE WIND

from Walt Disney's POCAHONTAS

Music by ALAN MENKEN
Lyrics by STEPHEN SCHWARTZ

DORA THE EXPLORER THEME SONG

from DORA THE EXPLORER

Words and Music by JOSH SITRON,
SARAH DURKEE and WILLIAM STRAUS

Bright Salsa feel

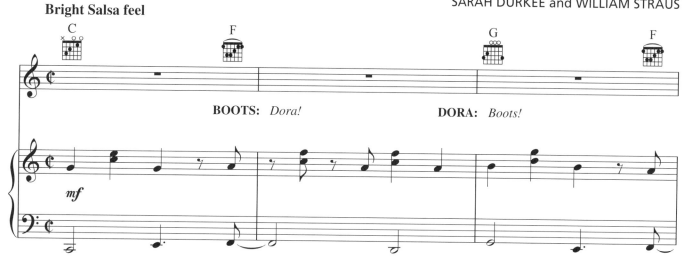

BOOTS: *Dora!*

DORA: *Boots!*

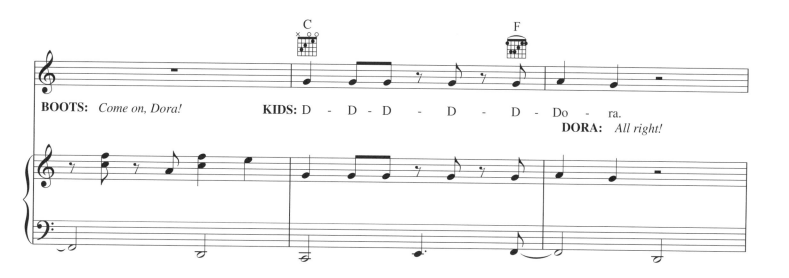

BOOTS: *Come on, Dora!*

KIDS: D - D - D - D - D - Do - ra.

DORA: *All right!*

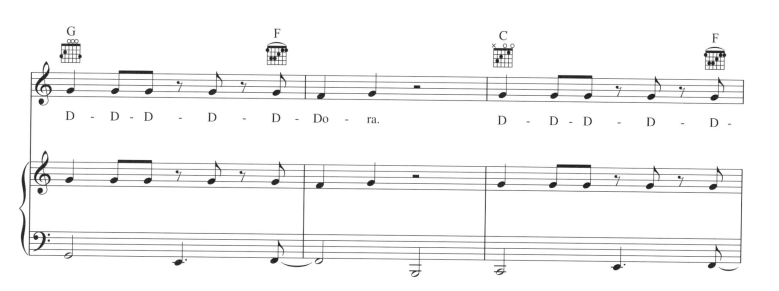

D - D - D - D - D - Do - ra.

D - D - D - D - D -

CONSIDER YOURSELF

from the Columbia Pictures - Romulus Motion Picture Production of Lionel Bart's OLIVER!

Words and Music by
LIONEL BART

DAY-O
(The Banana Boat Song)

Words and Music by IRVING BURGIE
and WILLIAM ATTAWAY

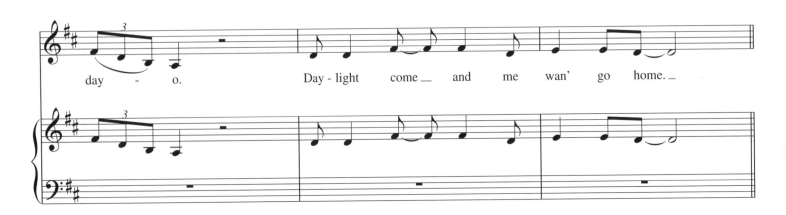

To Coda

DO-RE-MI

from THE SOUND OF MUSIC

Lyrics by OSCAR HAMMERSTEIN II
Music by RICHARD RODGERS

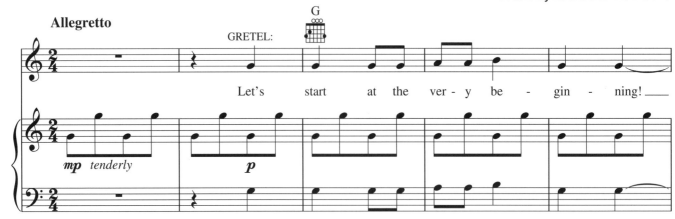

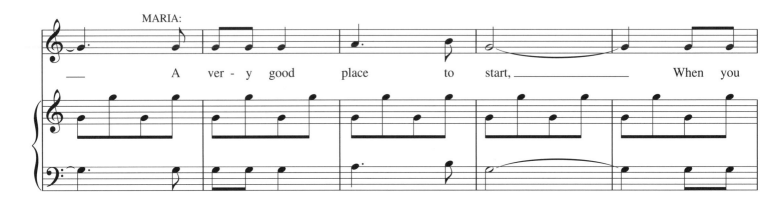

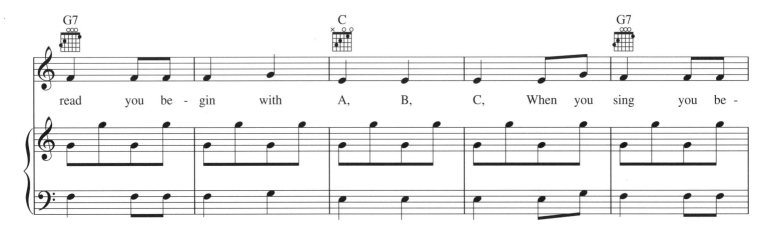

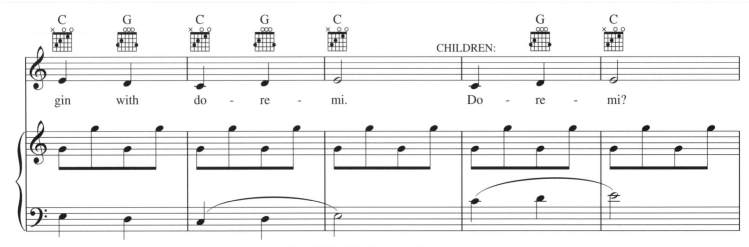

DOWN ON GRANDPA'S FARM

Traditional

Oh, we're on our way, we're on our way, on our way to Grand-pa's farm.

We're on our way, we're on our way, on our way to Grand-pa's farm.

Fine

farm.

1. Down on Grand-pa's farm there is a big brown
2. Down on Grand-pa's farm there is a lit - tle red
3. Down on Grand-pa's farm there is a big black
4.-7. *(See additional lyrics)*

Additional Lyrics

4. Down on Grandpa's farm there is a funny white duck.
   Down on Grandpa's farm there is a funny white duck.
   The duck, she makes a sound like this: quack, quack!
   The duck, she makes a sound like this: quack, quack!

5. Down on Grandpa's farm there is a fat pink pig.
   Down on Grandpa's farm there is a fat pink pig.
   The pig, she makes a sound like this: oink, oink!
   The pig, she makes a sound like this: oink, oink!

6. Down on Grandpa's farm there is a big brown horse.
   Down on Grandpa's farm there is a big brown horse.
   The horse, he makes a sound like this: neigh, neigh!
   The horse, he makes a sound like this: neigh, neigh!

7. Down on Grandpa's farm there is a new spring lamb.
   Down on Grandpa's farm there is a new spring lamb.
   The lamb, she makes a sound like this: baa, baa!
   The lamb, she makes a sound like this: baa, baa!

A DREAM IS A WISH YOUR HEART MAKES

from Walt Disney's CINDERELLA

Words and Music by MACK DAVID,
AL HOFFMAN and JERRY LIVINGSTON

EDELWEISS
from THE SOUND OF MUSIC

Lyrics by OSCAR HAMMERSTEIN II
Music by RICHARD RODGERS

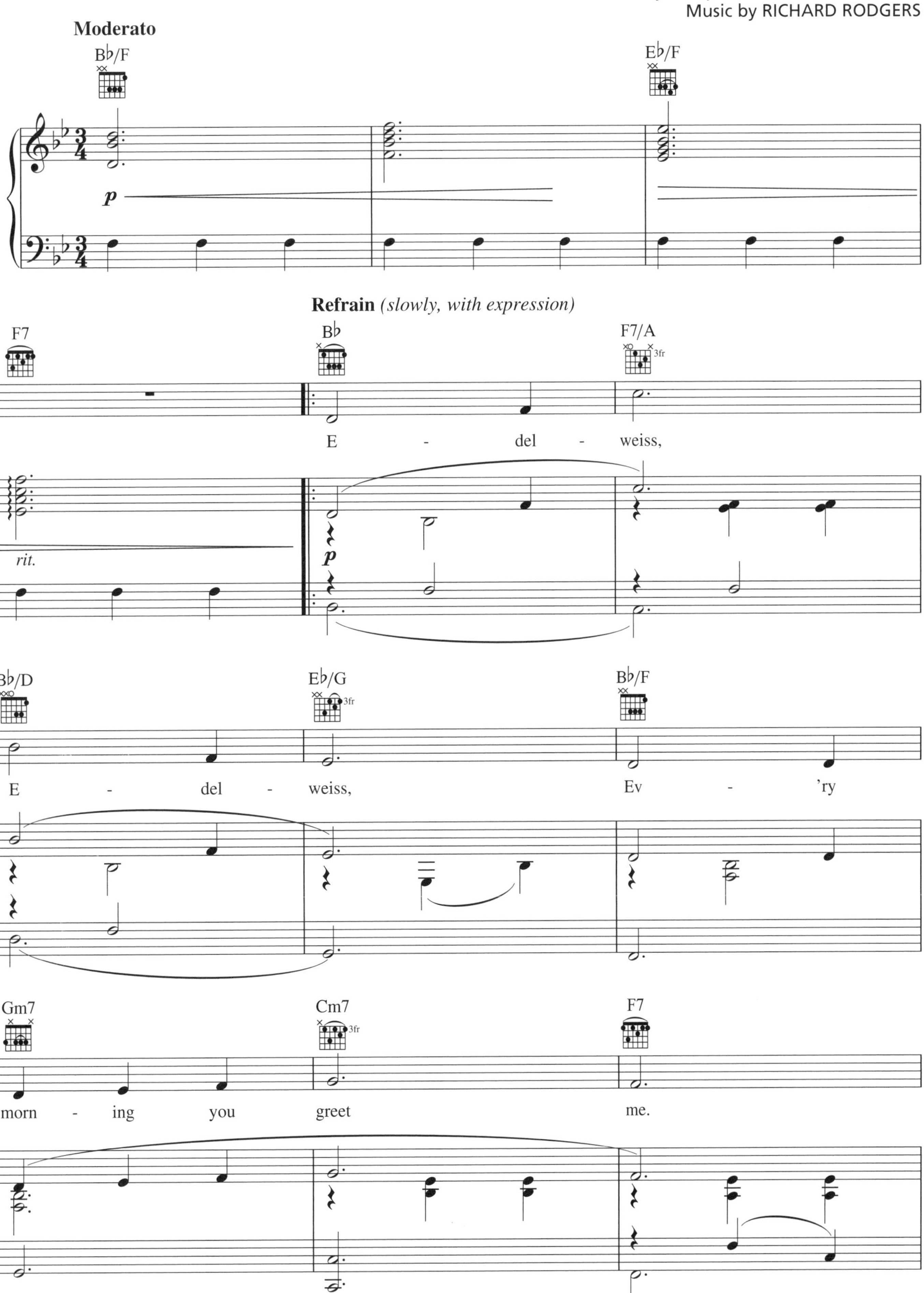

Moderato

Refrain (*slowly, with expression*)

E - del - weiss,

E - del - weiss,   Ev - 'ry

morn - ing you greet   me.

EVERYTHING IS BEAUTIFUL

Words and Music by
RAY STEVENS

Additional Lyrics

2. We shouldn't care about the length of his hair or the color of his skin,
Don't worry about what shows from without but the love that lies within,
We gonna get it all together now and everything gonna work out fine,
Just take a little time to look on the good side, my friend, and straighten it out in your mind.

FRIEND LIKE ME
from Walt Disney's ALADDIN

Words by HOWARD ASHMAN
Music by ALAN MENKEN

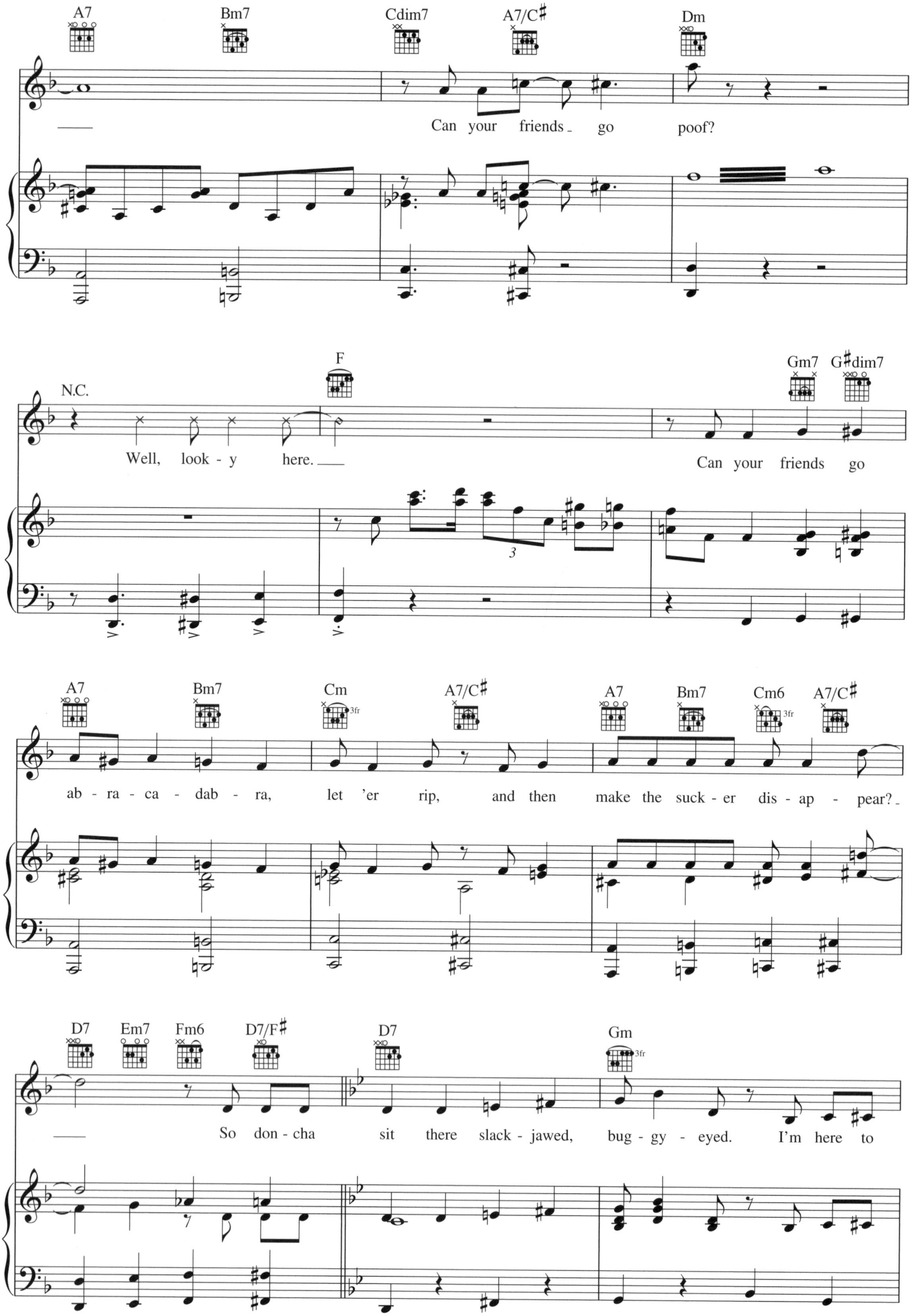

GIVE A LITTLE WHISTLE
from Walt Disney's PINOCCHIO

Words by NED WASHINGTON
Music by LEIGH HARLINE

When you get in trou-ble and you don't know right from wrong;
When you meet temp-ta-tion, and the urge is ver-y strong;
Give a lit-tle

whis-tle! (Whistle ___) Give a lit-tle whis-tle! (Whistle ___)

___) Not just a lit-tle squeak; Puck-er up and

GO TELL AUNT RHODY

Traditional

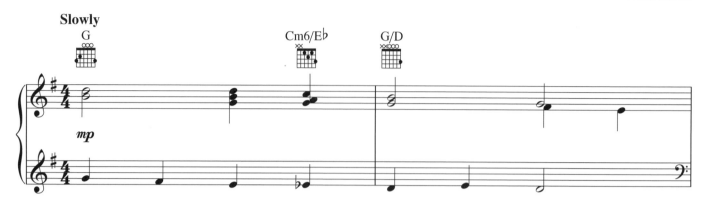

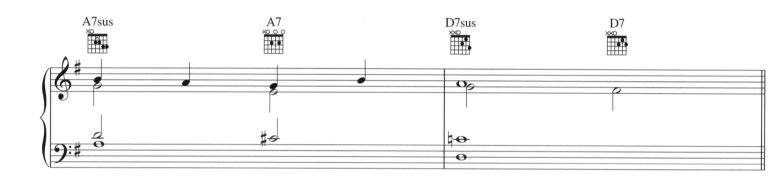

1. Go tell Aunt Rho - dy,
2.-5. *(See additional lyrics)*

131

Additional Lyrics

2. The one she was saving, *(three times)*
   To make a feather bed.

3. The gander is weeping, *(three times)*
   Because his wife is dead.

4. The goslings are crying, *(three times)*
   Because their mama's dead.

5. She died in the water, *(three times)*
   With her heels above her head.

HAPPY TRAILS

from the Television Series THE ROY ROGERS SHOW

Words and Music by
DALE EVANS

GOODBYE, OLD PAINT

Western American Cowboy Song

HEART AND SOUL
from the Paramount Short Subject A SONG IS BORN

Words by FRANK LOESSER
Music by HOAGY CARMICHAEL

Moderately, lightly rhythmical

HELLO MUDDUH, HELLO FADDUH!

(A Letter from Camp)

Words and Music by ALLAN SHERMAN
and LOU BUSCH

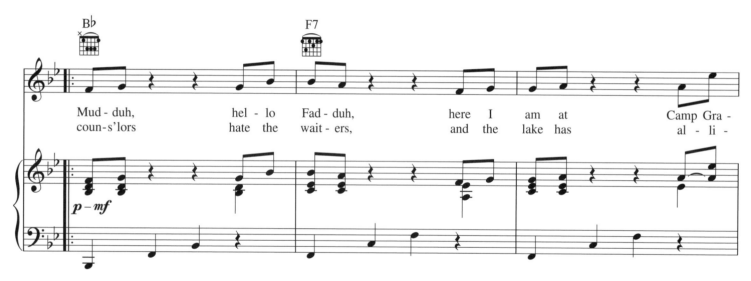

THE HOKEY POKEY

Words and Music by CHARLES P. MACAK,
TAFFT BAKER and LARRY LaPRISE

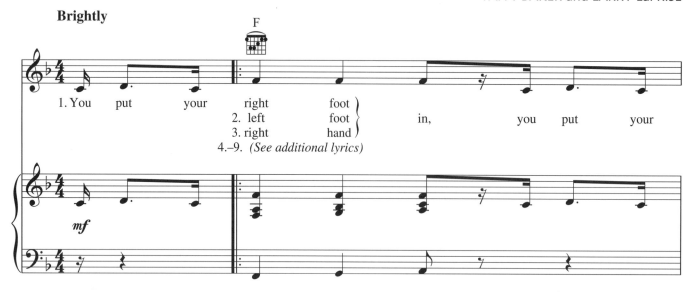

turn your - self a - bout. That's what it's all a -

bout.   Hey,   you put your   bout.   Hey!

Additional Lyrics

4. Hey, you put your left hand in,
   You put your left hand out.
   You put your left hand in,
   And you shake it all about.
   Chorus

5. Hey, you put your right shoulder in,
   You put your right shoulder out.
   You put your right shoulder in,
   And you shake it all about.
   Chorus

6. Hey, you put your left shoulder in,
   You put your left shoulder out.
   You put your left shoulder in,
   And you shake it all about.
   Chorus

7. Hey, you put your right hip in,
   You put your right hip out.
   You put your right hip in,
   And you shake it all about.
   Chorus

8. Hey, you put your left hip in,
   You put your left hip out.
   You put your left hip in,
   And you shake it all about.
   Chorus

9. Hey, you put your whole self in,
   You put your whole self out.
   You put your whole self in,
   And you shake it all about.
   Chorus

HOME ON THE RANGE

Lyrics by DR. BREWSTER HIGLEY
Music by DAN KELLY

1. Oh, give me a home where the
2. of- ten at night where when the
3.,4. *See additional lyrics*

buf- fa- lo roam, where the deer and the
heav- ens are bright, where from the light of the

an- te- lope play, where
glit- ter- ing stars, have I

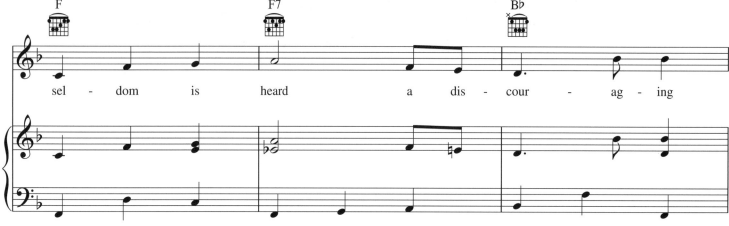

sel - dom is heard a dis - cour - ag - ing

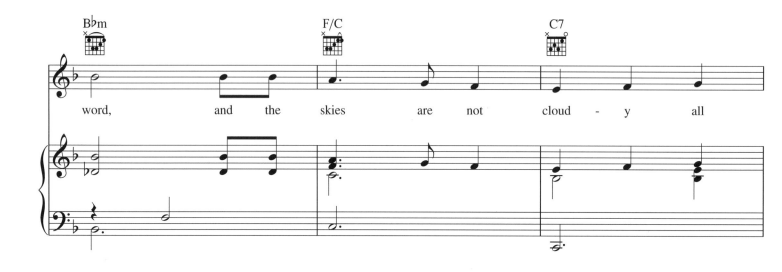

word, and the skies are not cloud - y all

day. _____

2. How
3. Where the day. _____
4. Oh,

rit. e dim.

p

Additional Lyrics

3. Where the air is so pure and the zephyrs so free,
And the breezes so balmy and light;
Oh, I would not exchange my home on the range
For the glittering cities so bright.
Chorus

4. Oh, give me a land where the bright diamond sand
Flows leisurely down with the stream,
Where the graceful white swan glides slowly along,
Like a maid in a heavenly dream.
Chorus

HOW MUCH IS THAT DOGGIE IN THE WINDOW

Words and Music by
BOB MERRILL

How much is that dog-gie in the win-dow? _____

(Bark, bark!)

The one with the wag-gel-y tail; _____ how much is that dog-gie in the

THE HUCKLEBUCK

Lyrics by ROY ALFRED
Music by ANDY GIBSON

I LOVE TRASH

from the Television Series SESAME STREET

Words and Music by
JEFF MOSS

I ENJOY BEING A GIRL

from FLOWER DRUM SONG

Lyrics by OSCAR HAMMERSTEIN II
Music by RICHARD RODGERS

I GAVE MY LOVE A CHERRY
(The Riddle Song)

Traditional

(I Scream — You Scream — We All Scream For)
ICE CREAM

Words and Music by HOWARD JOHNSON,
BILLY MOLL and ROBERT KING

In the land of ice and snows up a-mong the Es-ki-mos
Col-leg-es may come and go but the world will nev-er know

there's a col-lege known as Oo-gie-wa-wa. (Wa-wa-wa)
an-y oth-er place like Oo-gie-wa-wa. (Wa-wa-wa)

I WHISTLE A HAPPY TUNE

from THE KING AND I

Lyrics by OSCAR HAMMERSTEIN II
Music by RICHARD RODGERS

Whistle

are.

You may be as

brave

as you make be - lieve you

are.

pp

8va

p

I'VE GOT NO STRINGS

from Walt Disney's PINOCCHIO

Words by NED WASHINGTON
Music by LEIGH HARLINE

I WON'T GROW UP

from PETER PAN

Lyric by CAROLYN LEIGH
Music by MARK CHARLAP

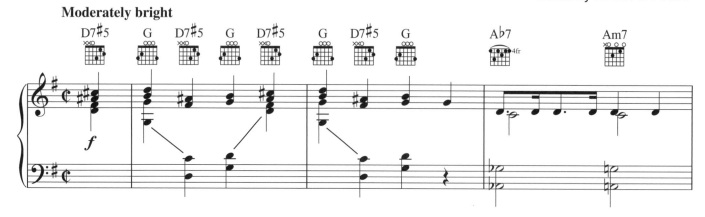

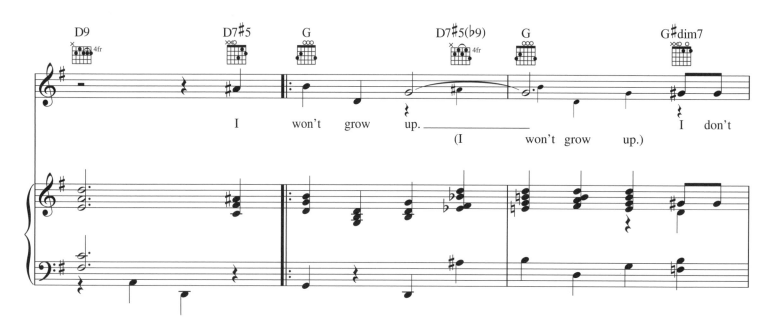

I'M LATE

from Walt Disney's ALICE IN WONDERLAND

Words by BOB HILLIARD
Music by SAMMY FAIN

Brightly

I'm late, I'm late for a ver-y im-por-tant date. No

time to say hel - lo, good - bye, I'm late, I'm late, I'm late, I'm late, and

when I wave, I lose the time I save. My fuzz-y ears and

IF I NEVER KNEW YOU
(Love Theme from POCAHONTAS)
from Walt Disney's POCAHONTAS

Music by ALAN MENKEN
Lyrics by STEPHEN SCHWARTZ

Male: If I nev - er knew you, ___

IT'S A SMALL WORLD

from Disneyland Resort® and Magic Kingdom® Park

Words and Music by RICHARD M. SHERMAN
and ROBERT B. SHERMAN

It's a world of laugh - ter, a
just one moon and one

world of tears; it's a world of hopes and a
gold - en sun, and a smile means friend - ship to

KISS THE GIRL
from Walt Disney's THE LITTLE MERMAID

Lyrics by HOWARD ASHMAN
Music by ALAN MENKEN

LET THERE BE PEACE ON EARTH

Words and Music by SY MILLER
and JILL JACKSON

KUM BA YAH

Traditional Spiritual

LINUS AND LUCY

By VINCE GUARALDI

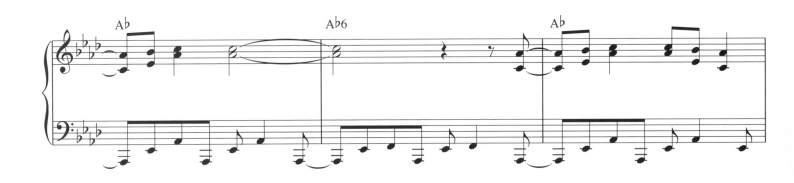

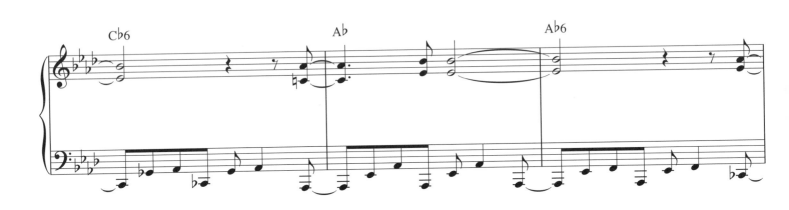

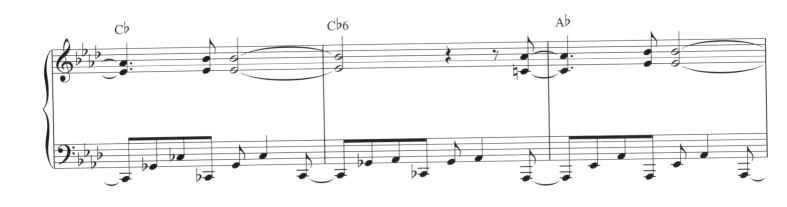

LITTLE APRIL SHOWER

from Walt Disney's BAMBI

Words by LARRY MOREY
Music by FRANK CHURCHILL

Brightly and lightly

I nev-er mind how much it rains in A - pril.

I nev-er lose my tem-per and com - plain. If

you come down my way on an-y rain-y day, you'll

LITTLE PEOPLE

from LES MISÉRABLES

Music by CLAUDE-MICHEL SCHÖNBERG
Lyrics by ALAIN BOUBLIL, JEAN-MARC NATEL
and HERBERT KRETZMER

may look eas-y pick-ings but we got some bite! So nev-er kick a dog be-cause it's just a pup. You bet-ter run for cov-er when the pup grows up! And we'll fight like twen-ty ar-mies and we won't give up! A

D.S. al Coda

CODA

flea can bite the bot-tom of the Pope in Rome!

MAGIC PENNY

Words and Music by
MALVINA REYNOLDS

THE LORD IS GOOD TO ME

from Walt Disney's MELODY TIME

Words and Music by KIM GANNON
and WALTER KENT

MAH-NÁ MAH-NÁ

By PIERO UMILIANI

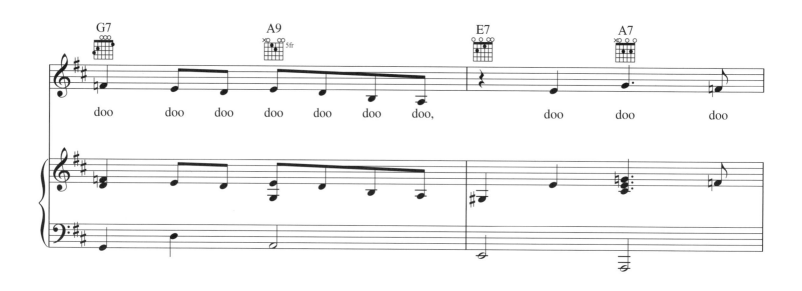

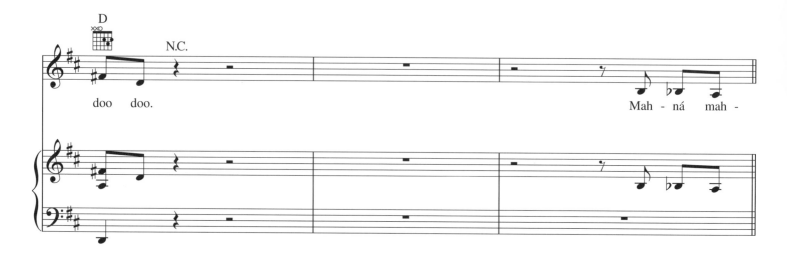

MAIRZY DOATS

Words and Music by MILTON DRAKE,
AL HOFFMAN and JERRY LIVINGSTON

OH WHERE, OH WHERE HAS MY LITTLE DOG GONE

Words by SEP. WININER
Traditional Melody

Oh where, oh where has my lit-tle dog gone? Oh where, oh

where can he be? _____ With his ears cut short and his

tail cut long; oh where, oh where can he be? _____

MICKEY MOUSE MARCH
from Walt Disney's THE MICKEY MOUSE CLUB

Words and Music by
JIMMIE DODD

NEVER SMILE AT A CROCODILE

from Walt Disney's PETER PAN

Words by JACK LAWRENCE
Music by FRANK CHURCHILL

OLD DAN TUCKER

Traditional

1. Went to town the oth-er night, to hear a noise and see a fight.
2. Old Dan Tuck-er's a fine old man, ___ washed his face in a fry-ing pan.
3. Old Dan Tuck-er came to town, ___ rid-ing a bil-ly goat, lead-ing a hound.
4.-6. *(See additional lyrics)*

All the peo-ple were run-ning a-round say-ing old Dan Tuck-er's come to town.
Combed his hair with a wag-on wheel and died with a tooth-ache in his heel.
Hound barked and the bil-ly goat jumped; throwed old Dan right strad-dle of a stump.

Chorus

Get out the way, old Dan Tuck - er, you're too late to come for sup - per.

Sup - per's o - ver and din - ner's cook - ing and old Dan Tuck - er just stand - ing there look - ing.

Additional Lyrics

4. Old Dan Tucker clumb a tree,
His Lord and Master for to see.
The limb it broke and Dan got a fall.
Never got to see his Lord at all.
Chorus

5. Old Dan Tucker he got drunk,
Fell in the fire and he kicked up a chunk;
Red hot coal got in his shoe,
Lord God-amighty how the ashes flew!
Chorus

6. Old Dan Tucker he come to town,
Swinging the ladies 'round and 'round,
First to the right and then to the left,
And then to the one that you love the best.
Chorus

ONCE UPON A DREAM

from Walt Disney's SLEEPING BEAUTY

Words and Music by SAMMY FAIN
and JACK LAWRENCE
Adapted from a Theme by TCHAIKOVSKY

ONE SMALL VOICE
from the Television Series SESAME STREET

Words and Music by
JEFF MOSS

Moderately

Ev - 'ry song the world sings, each was once un-
No tune is too sim - ple. No voice once can be

known. Some - bod - y felt a song in - side and
wrong. Mu - sic can come from an - y heart and

was - n't a - fraid to sing a - lone. ___ If you feel the
an - y - one's voice can lead the song. ___ If you feel the

RED RIVER VALLEY

Traditional American Cowboy Song

Slowly

From this val - ley they say you are go - ing, _____ you are chang - ing your range for a
sit here a - while ere you leave us, _____ do not has - ten to bid us a -

while. So you say you are wea - ry and ti - red; _____ we shall
dieu. Come back soon to the Red Riv - er Val - ley, _____ and the

miss your dear face and your smile. Then come true.
cow - boy who loves you so

PEOPLE IN YOUR NEIGHBORHOOD

from the Television Series SESAME STREET

Words and Music by
JEFF MOSS

PERFECT WORLD
from Walt Disney Pictures' THE EMPEROR'S NEW GROOVE

Lyrics by STING
Music by STING and DAVID HARTLEY

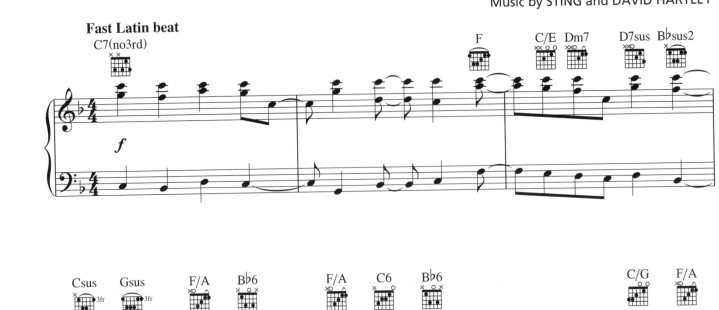

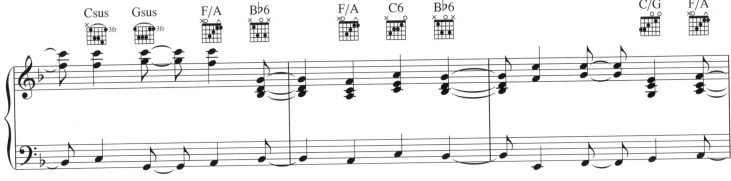

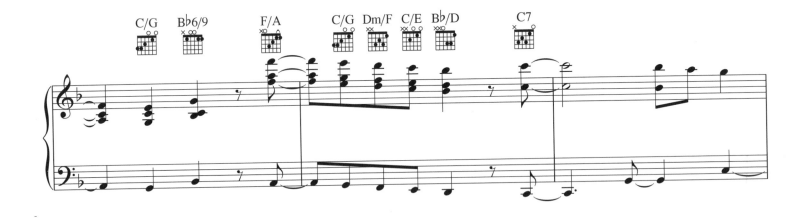

PUFF THE MAGIC DRAGON

Words and Music by LENNY LIPTON
and PETER YARROW

*3rd time, play verse twice
before proceeding to Chorus

Additional Lyrics

2. Together they would travel on a boat with billowed sail.
   Jackie kept a lookout perched on Puff's gigantic tail.
   Noble kings and princes would bow when e'er they came.
   Pirate ships would low'r their flags when Puff roared out his name. Oh!
   (Chorus)

3. A dragon lives forever, but not so little boys.
   Painted wings and giant rings make way for other toys.
   One gray night it happened, Jackie Paper came no more,
   And Puff that mighty dragon, he ceased his fearless roar.

4. His head was bent in sorrow, green tears fell like rain.
   Puff no longer went to play along the Cherry Lane.
   Without his lifelong friend, Puff could not be brave,
   So Puff that mighty dragon sadly slipped into his cave. Oh!
   (Chorus)

*THE RETURN OF PUFF

5. Puff the magic dragon danced down the Cherry Lane.
   He came upon a little girl, Julie Maple was her name.
   She'd heard that Puff had gone away, but that can never be,
   So together they went sailing to the land called Honalee.
   (Chorus)

PURPLE PEOPLE EATER

Words and Music by
SHEB WOOLEY

Additional Lyrics

3. I said, "Mister purple people eater, what's your line?"
   He said, "Eatin' purple people, and it sure is fine,
   But that's not the reason that I came to land,
   I wanna get a job in a rock and roll band."
   Chorus

4. And then he swung from the tree and he lit on the ground,
   And he started to rock, a-really rockin' around.
   It was a crazy ditty with a swingin' tune,
   Singa bop bapa loop a lap a loom bam boom.
   Chorus

5. Well, he went on his way and then what-a you know,
   I saw him last night on a TV show,
   He was blowin' it out, really knockin' 'em dead,
   Playin' rock 'n' roll music thru the horn in his head.
   Chorus

RUBBER DUCKIE
from the Television Series SESAME STREET

Words and Music by
JEFF MOSS

Moderately bright

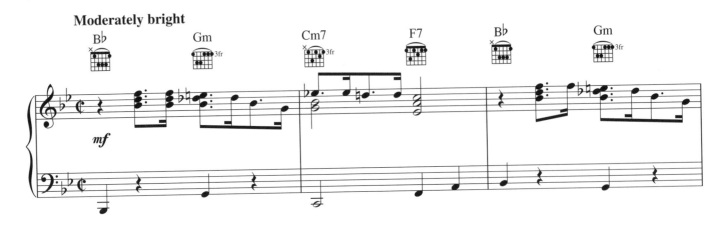

Rub - ber Duck - ie, you're the one,

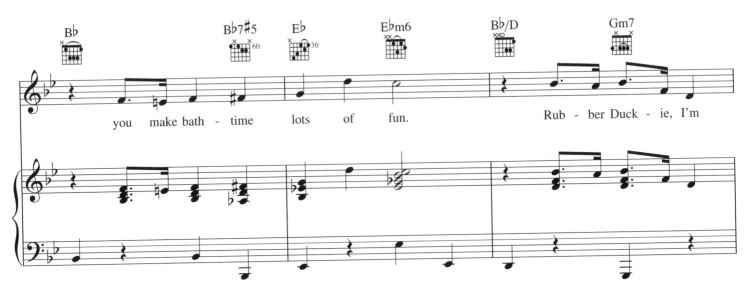

you make bath - time lots of fun. Rub - ber Duck - ie, I'm

SCALES AND ARPEGGIOS

from Walt Disney's THE ARISTOCATS

Words and Music by RICHARD M. SHERMAN
and ROBERT B. SHERMAN

Do mi so do do so mi do.

Ev - 'ry tru - ly cul - tured mu - sic stu - dent knows
If you're faith - ful to your dai - ly prac - tic - ing,
Though at first it seems as tho' it does - n't show,

you must learn your scales and your ar - peg - gi - os.
you will find your pro - gress is en - cour - ag - ing.
like a tree, a - bil - i - ty will bloom and grow.

Do mi so do do so mi do. Do mi so do do so mi do.

D.S. al Coda

ev - 'ry art - ist knows: you must sing your scales and your ar - peg - gi -

os.

THE SECOND STAR TO THE RIGHT

from Walt Disney's PETER PAN

Words by SAMMY CAHN
Music by SAMMY FAIN

Moderately slow

The sec-ond star to the right shines in the night for you,

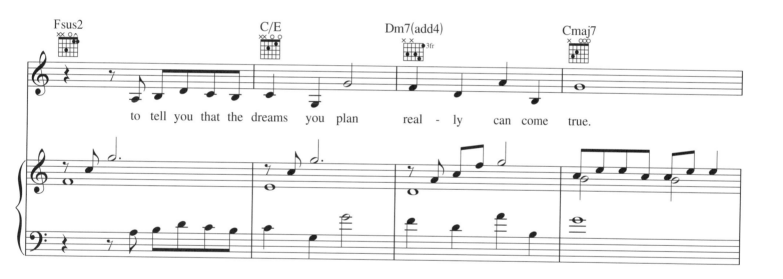

to tell you that the dreams you plan real-ly can come true.

The sec-ond star to the right shines with a light that's

SCHOOL DAYS
(When We Were a Couple of Kids)

Words by WILL D. COBB
Music by GUS EDWARDS

SESAME STREET THEME

Words by BRUCE HART,
JON STONE and JOE RAPOSO
Music by JOE RAPOSO

THE SOUND OF MUSIC

from THE SOUND OF MUSIC

Lyrics by OSCAR HAMMERSTEIN II
Music by RICHARD RODGERS

Molto moderato *(tenderly)*

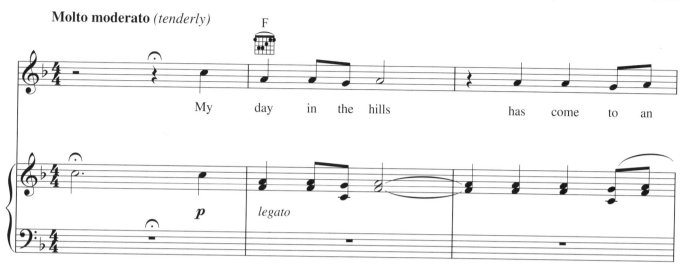

My day in the hills has come to an

end, I know. A star has come out to tell me it's

time to go. But deep in the dark green shad-ows are

voic - es that urge me to stay. So I pause and I wait and I

lis - ten for one more sound, For one more love-ly thing that the hills might

Refrain (*moderately, with warm expression*)

say. The hills are a-live with the sound of mu - sic, ___

With songs they have sung for a thou - sand years. ___

SING
from SESAME STREET

Words and Music by
JOE RAPOSO

SOME DAY MY PRINCE WILL COME

from Walt Disney's SNOW WHITE AND THE SEVEN DWARFS

Words by LARRY MOREY
Music by FRANK CHURCHILL

Some day my prince will come, Some
Some day I'll find my love,

day I'll find my love, and how thrill-ing that
one to call my own, and how I'll know her the

mo-ment will be, _____ When the prince of my dreams comes to
mo-ment we meet, _____ For my heart will start skip-ping a

SPONGEBOB SQUAREPANTS THEME SONG

from SPONGEBOB SQUAREPANTS

Words and Music by MARK HARRISON,
BLAISE SMITH, STEVE HILLENBURG
and DEREK DRYMON

Moderately fast

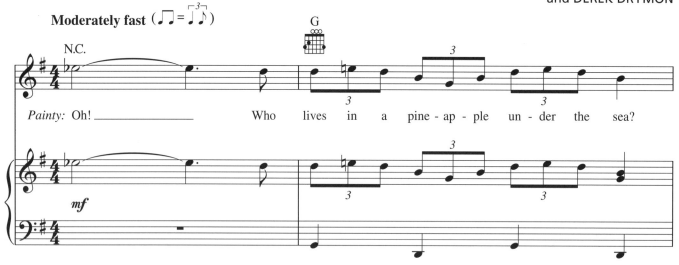

Painty: Oh! _____ Who lives in a pine-ap-ple un-der the sea?

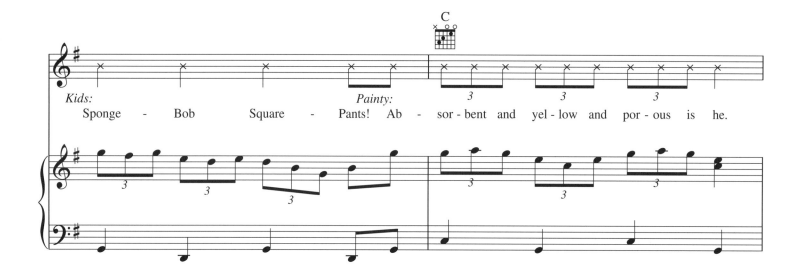

Kids: Sponge - Bob Square - Pants! *Painty:* Ab - sor-bent and yel-low and por-ous is he.

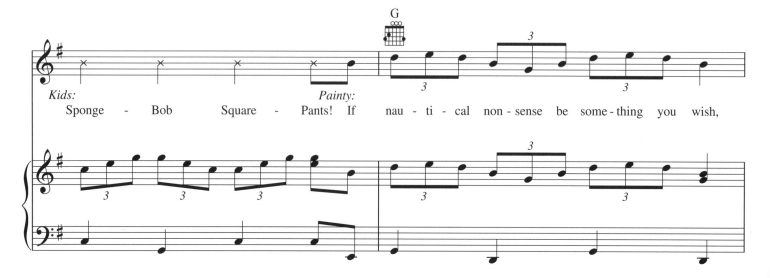

Kids: Sponge - Bob Square - Pants! *Painty:* If nau-ti-cal non-sense be some-thing you wish,

TOGETHER FOREVER

from ELMO IN GROUCHLAND

Words and Music by MICHAEL SILVERSHER
and PATTY SILVERSHER

THERE'S A HOLE IN THE BUCKET

Traditional

Additional Lyrics

3. With what shall I fix it, dear Liza, etc.
4. With a straw, dear Henry, etc.
5. But the straw is too long, dear Liza, etc.
6. Then cut it, dear Henry, etc.
7. With what shall I cut it, dear Liza, etc.
8. With a knife, dear Henry, etc.
9. But the knife is too dull, Dear Liza, etc.
10. Then sharpen it, dear Liza, etc.

11. With what shall I sharpen it, dear Liza, etc.
12. With a stone, dear Henry, etc.
13. But the stone is too dry, dear Liza, etc.
14. Then wet it, dear Henry, etc.
15. With what shall I wet it, dear Liza, etc.
16. With water, dear Henry, etc.
17. In what shall I carry it, dear Liza, etc.
18. In a bucket, dear Henry, etc.

19. There's a hole in the bucket, dear Liza, etc.

THIS LAND IS YOUR LAND

Words and Music by
WOODY GUTHRIE

Bright and cheerful

As I went

(1.) walk - ing _____ that rib - bon of high - way _____ I saw a -
(2.,4.,6.) your land, _____ this land is my land, _____ from Cal - i -
(3.) ram - bled _____ and I fol-lowed my foot - steps _____ to the spar - kling
(5.) shin - ing, _____ and I was stroll - ing; _____ the wheat fields

bove me _____ that end - less sky - way; _____ I saw be -
for - nia _____ to the New York is - land; _____ from the red - wood
sands of _____ her dia - mond des - erts; _____ while all a -
wav - ing _____ and the dust clouds roll - ing. _____ The fog was

THIS TRAIN

Traditional

1. This train is bound for glo - ry, this train. _____
2.-6. *(See additional lyrics)*

This train is bound for glo - ry, this train. _____ This train is

Additional Lyrics

2. This train don't carry no gamblers, *(3 times)*
   No hypocrites, no midnight ramblers,
   This train is bound for glory, this train.

3. This train don't carry no liars, *(3 times)*
   No hypocrites and no high flyers,
   This train is bound for glory, this train.

4. This train is built for speed now, *(3 times)*
   Fastest train you ever did see,
   This train is bound for glory, this train.

5. This train you don't pay no transportation, *(3 times)*
   No Jim Crow and no discrimination,
   This train is bound for glory, this train.

6. This train don't carry no rustlers, *(3 times)*
   Sidestreet walkers, two-bit hustlers,
   This train is bound for glory, this train.

TOMORROW

from the Musical Production ANNIE

Lyric by MARTIN CHARNIN
Music by CHARLES STROUSE

The sun - 'll come out ____ to - mor - row,

bet your bot - tom dol - lar that to - mor - row ____ there'll be

sun! Jus' think - ing a - bout ____ to - mor - row

THE UNBIRTHDAY SONG

from Walt Disney's ALICE IN WONDERLAND

Words by and Music by MACK DAVID,
AL HOFFMAN and JERRY LIVINGSTON

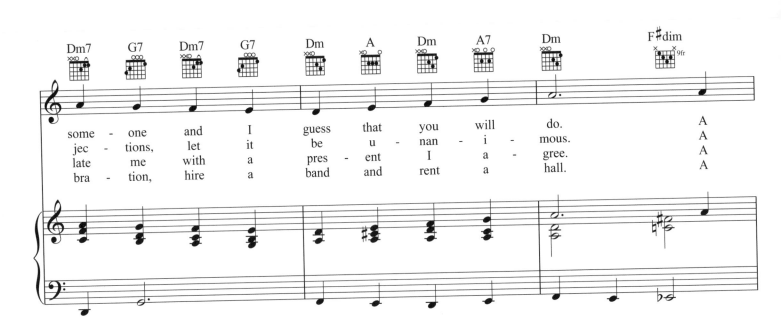

TOYLAND
from BABES IN TOYLAND

Words by GLEN MacDONOUGH
Music by VICTOR HERBERT

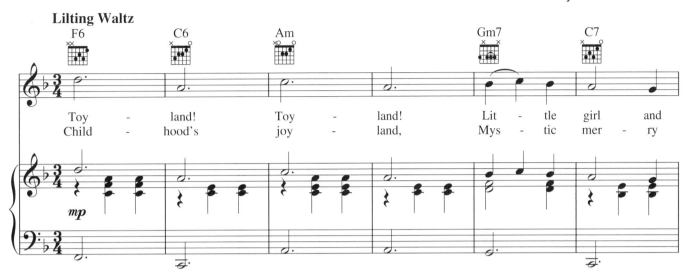

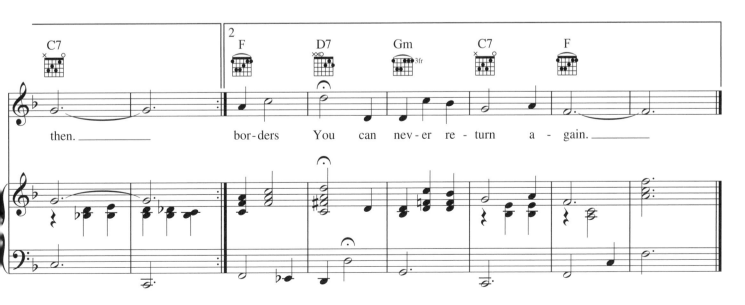

VEGGIETALES THEME SONG

Words and Music by MIKE NAWROCKI
and LISA VISCHER

Bob: If you like to talk to to-ma-toes, if a squash can make you smile, if you like to waltz with po-ta-toes up and down the pro-duce aisle... *Have we got a show for you!*

March tempo

WE'RE ALL IN THIS TOGETHER

from the Disney Channel Original Movie HIGH SCHOOL MUSICAL

Words and Music by MATTHEW GERRARD
and ROBBIE NEVIL

*Recorded a half step lower.

328

A WHALE OF A TALE

from Walt Disney's 20,000 LEAGUES UNDER THE SEA

Words and Music by NORMAN GIMBEL
and AL HOFFMAN

WHEN JOHNNY COMES MARCHING HOME

Words and Music by
PATRICK SARSFIELD GILMORE

WHEN YOU BELIEVE

(From THE PRINCE OF EGYPT)

Words and Music by STEPHEN SCHWARTZ
with Additional Music by BABYFACE

Man-y nights we've prayed, with no proof an-y-one could hear.

In our hearts a hope-ful song _ we bare-ly un-der-stood. Now

we are not _ a-fraid, al-though we know there's much to fear.

WHEN YOU WISH UPON A STAR

from Walt Disney's PINOCCHIO

Words by NED WASHINGTON
Music by LEIGH HARLINE

When a star is born, They pos-sess a gift or two,

One of them is this: They have the pow-er____ to make a wish come true.

When you wish up-on a star, makes no diff-'rence

WHISTLE WHILE YOU WORK

from Walt Disney's SNOW WHITE AND THE SEVEN DWARFS

Words by LARRY MOREY
Music by FRANK CHURCHILL

Brightly

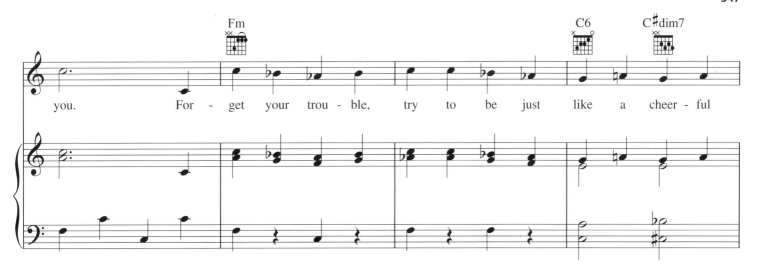

you. For - get your trou - ble, try to be just like a cheer - ful

chick - a - dee. And whis - tle while you work. *(whistle)* _____ Come

on, get smart, tune up and start to whis - tle while you work.

WHO'S AFRAID OF THE BIG BAD WOLF?

from Walt Disney's THREE LITTLE PIGS

Words and Music by FRANK CHURCHILL
Additional lyric by ANN RONELL

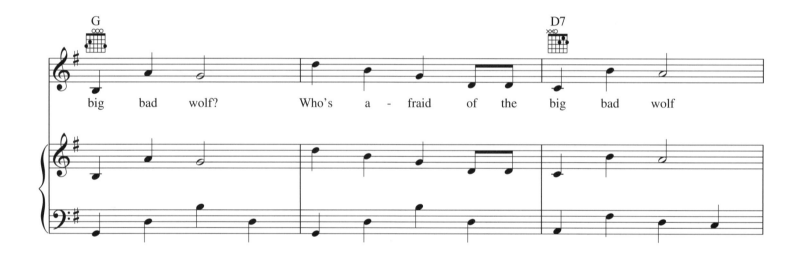

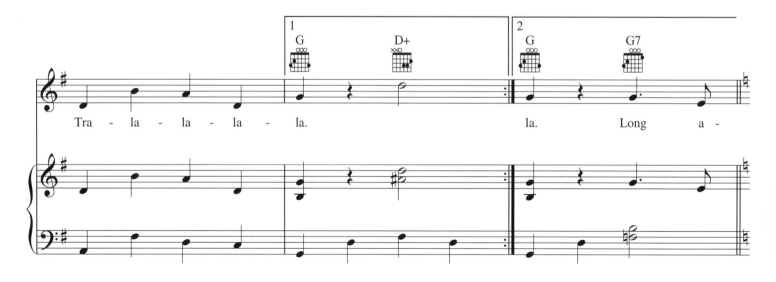

YOU'LL BE IN MY HEART

(Pop Version)

from Walt Disney Pictures' TARZAN™

Words and Music by
PHIL COLLINS

WON'T YOU BE MY NEIGHBOR?
(It's a Beautiful Day in the Neighborhood)
from MISTER ROGERS' NEIGHBORHOOD

Words and Music by
FRED ROGERS

YOU'RE A GRAND OLD FLAG

Words and Music by
GEORGE M. COHAN

YOU'VE GOT A FRIEND IN ME
from Walt Disney's TOY STORY

Music and Lyrics by
RANDY NEWMAN

ZIP-A-DEE-DOO-DAH

from Walt Disney's SONG OF THE SOUTH

Words by RAY GILBERT
Music by ALLIE WRUBEL

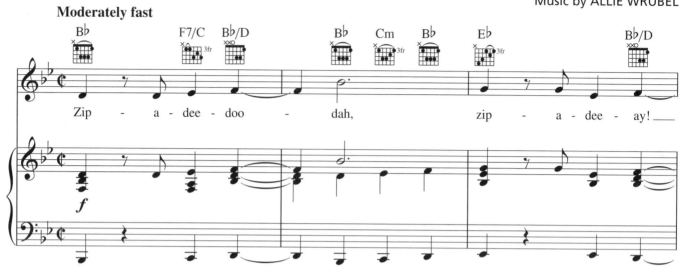

Zip - a-dee-doo - dah, zip - a-dee-ay!

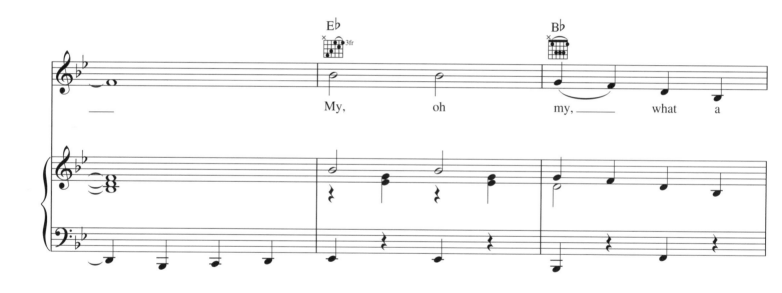

My, oh my, ____ what a

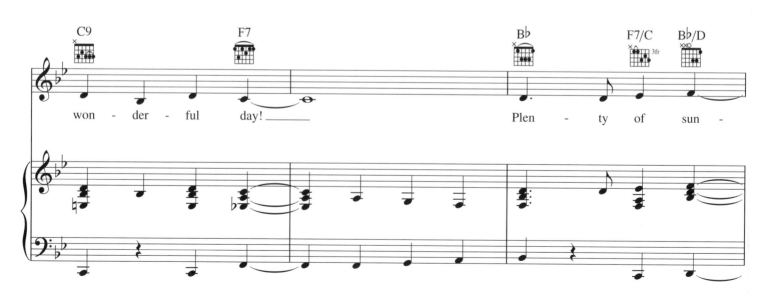

won - der - ful day! ____ Plen - ty of sun -